ADAMANTINE

ADAMANTINE

poems

Naomi Foyle

Pighog Press

Book design by Mark E. Cull
Cover photograph by Fabio Sozza

Library of Congress Cataloging-in-Publication Data

Names: Foyle, Naomi, author.
Title: Adamantine : poems / Naomi Foyle.
Description: First edition. | Pasadena, CA : Pighog Press, [2019] |
    Identifiers: LCCN 2019017801 (print) | LCCN 2019018689 (ebook) | ISBN
    9781906309473 (ebook) | ISBN 9781906309411 (print)
Classification: LCC PR6106.O965 (ebook) | LCC PR6106.O965 A6 2019 (print) |
    DDC 821/.92—dc23
LC record available at https://lccn.loc.gov/2019017801

The National Endowment for the Arts, the Los Angeles County Arts Commission, the
Ahmanson Foundation, the Dwight Stuart Youth Fund, the Max Factor Family Foundation,
the Pasadena Tournament of Roses Foundation, the Pasadena Arts & Culture Commission
and the City of Pasadena Cultural Affairs Division, the City of Los Angeles Department of
Cultural Affairs, the Audrey & Sydney Irmas Charitable Foundation, the Kinder Morgan
Foundation, the Meta & George Rosenberg Foundation, the Allergan Foundation, and the
Riordan Foundation all partially support Red Hen Press.

First Edition
Pighog Press is an imprint of Red Hen Press, Pasadena, CA, USA
www.redhen.org/pighog

Acknowledgements

Heartfelt thanks to Kate Gale, Mark E. Cull and their crack team at Red Hen Press for bringing this book into being. Many of the poems in the first section were written as part of my PhD thesis for Bangor University, under the inspiriting supervision of Carol Rumens. I am grateful to the Arts and Humanities Research Council for funding my doctoral work and to the Francis W Reckitt Arts Trust for a grant that allowed me to revise these poems in the tranquil and visionary environs of Hawkwood College, Gloucestershire. I also thank the Royal Literary Society for two grants that supported me during periods of ill health in 2013 and 2017, the latter greatly enabling the writing of *The Cancer Breakthrough*.

Hugh Dunkerley, Sarah Hymas and Joanna Lowry all gave crucial feedback on work in progress, as did Rob Hamberger, who carefully critiqued the whole manuscript. I am indebted also to Farid S. Bitar, Haim Bresheeth, Moyra Donaldson, Fady Joudah, Yosefa Loshitsky, Peter Pegnall, Naomi Shihab Nye, Monica Suswin, Lee Whitaker and the members of A Casa dos Poetas 2017 for their thoughtful comments on particular poems.

Thanks are due to the editors of the following journals, in which some of these poems first appeared: *Ambit, Babylon Festival for International Cultures & Arts* newsletter, *Critical Muslim, Kalyna Review, London Grip, Poetry Salzburg Review, Poetry and All That Jazz, The Recusant* and *Rusted Radishes*.

Haringey Literature Live produced a spoken word podcast of 'Mama Africa', which can be heard at https://soundcloud.com/naomi-foyle/mama-africa. The Poetry Café at the Underground Theatre (Eastbourne) produced a live video recording of 'If It Is a War . . .' available on their Facebook page at https://www.facebook.com/poetrycafeugt.

'Eva Gore-Booth and Con Markievicz Gently Chide an Old Friend' and 'An Aisling' were previously published in the pamphlet *No Enemy but Time* (Waterloo Press, 2017).

A previous version of 'Shaking the Bottle' was shortlisted for the 2010 Academi Cardiff International Poetry Competition.

The epigraphical definitions of 'adamant' and 'adamantine' are taken from Wiktionary and the Oxford English Dictionary.

for Sarah Hymas

Contents

ADAMANTINE

THE CANCER BREAKTHROUGH

ADAMANTINE

adamant (*plural* **adamants**)

>   1. An imaginary rock or mineral of impenetrable hardness; a name given to the diamond and other substances of extreme hardness.
>   2. An embodiment of impregnable hardness.
>   3. A magnet; a lodestone.

adamantine

>   1. Made of adamant, or having the qualities of adamant; incapable of being broken, dissolved, or penetrated.
>   ***adamantine*** *bonds*
>   ***adamantine*** *chains*
>   2. Like the diamond in hardness or lustre.

[OF *adamaunt* f. L *adamas adamant-* untameable f. Gk (as A-, *damaō* to tame)]

ADAMANTINE

Two Emilys

after Emily Carr
i.m. Emily Givner

Odoodem poles.
She stared at them so long
that everything—forest, ocean, rain—
carved pathways to the infinite
kinship she craved.
                            Her sky
was a scraped oyster shell,
pearly shale rubbed raw.
Her trees swirl and bulge,
emerald, jade and lime
meringues she beat
until her arms were stiff,
folding in the dazzle
of the light beyond
the clouds.
But though
                    her paintings exude
the scent of cedar and sea,
capture the tilt of totems
from Cumshewa
to Gitanyow,
they cannot show you
the true height or shapes
of those poles,
nor the long shadows
of their meaning
in languages broken
like salamander bones.

ℰ

Emily—

my fierce high school friend,
Empress of impossible questions . . .
how fear twitched like a fish in my belly
when you'd swivel round in class to hiss:
"Would you go back in time and kill Hitler?"
or, when I was still a shy virgin,
"So, Ni. Would you have sex
with a black man?"

I backtracked and stalled.
You went hunting for answers—
not, like me, at university.
I glimpsed you before I left town,
sauntering down Albert St in a mini-skirt,
hand-in-hand with your Cree boyfriend,
sunlight licking the back of your legs,
a feather caressing your hair.

Small town girls with big dreams,
our paths should have criss-crossed later
in Toronto, Seoul, the wine-fuelled reunions
of prodigal daughters and journeying writers—
but you secretly suffered from allergies,
died without warning on a hot day in Halifax,
leaving so many conversations unfinished.

Emily, your spirit burned brighter
than a Saskatchewan summer;
your small face still shines
like the moon in my waters.

♇

Klee Wyck,
'the laughing one',
the Nuu-chah-nulth
named her,
offering Emily,
her dancing brushes,
elated paint,
a place
beneath the cedar ribs
of their ancestral longhouse,
a privileged spirit witness
to its blowhole of forbidden tradition:
the Pacific Northwest Coast's
ceremonial gift-giving feast.
But how can a white artist
circling around
that defiant exchange
of oolichan, canoes,
whale oil and sta-bigs,
ornamental coppers, sealskins
and Hudson Bay blankets,
not steal
away with the
power of her hosts?
Gnawed at by critics,
Carr's monumental status
teeters and sways
on a point of
heart
to
heart
contact
with the First People
of a country that banned the 'uncivilized' potlatch from 1884 to 1951.

౿

Sticky
as sap,
a poem
drips
down
the page.
Only
voiced
can it
soar
into
air.

Emily
wrote stories,
won a summer prize
for 'Canadian Mint',
her slyly spooky tale
of enterprising
Eddie,
sittin' out all day
on Bloor Street,
building pillars
from pennies . . .

an arcane way
to zigzag time
I researched
on the empty
shelves
of my first flat
in England,
but not a sight
I'd ever seen
on sidewalks—

until that August
morning, when,
back in Canada
at last, running
late to meet
Emily's parents
for the first time
since her death,

I thundered past
a woman kneeling
by a bus stop,
      cracking open
rolls of coins,
         a spilling
      wealth
of pennies

   to join the
copper forest
      growing
         on the concrete
      that for a silver
         moment
   disappeared
      beneath
         my flying
         feet

⤴

Zunoqua—
capricious spirit,
snatcher of children,
bestower of wealth—
your predatory breasts
thrust like cougars
through a forest
few European women
penetrate alone.
In the stillness
of a long-deserted
Gwat'sinux village,
Carr, at last, perceived you
as benign. And though
that towering carving
was in fact a male
ancestor of the Chief,
as Emily spread the dark
paint on her canvas
a dawn of feral cats,
eyes glinting
like gold planets,
came prowling
through the
undergrowth
to hiss she was
not entirely
wrong.

reQuesting

i.m. Pamela Jean George

How to return home
to a land I wasn't born in
a land my people took
from a people who know
that no-one owns the Earth
How to return
that land?

How to respond
to beadwork moccasins,
moosehair embroidery,
a porcupine quill Mickey Mouse,
to baskets woven so tightly
they could carry water
if they weren't
kept behind glass
in a museum?

Resurgent crafts?
Decorative arts? Tragic tat?
Or anonymous, needle-nimble expressions
of the one great human idea:
that we are all

c
o
n
n
e
c
t
e
d

all
hanging
by the same
spit-wet thread,
our uncommon colours
dyed and stitched
into the same
warm skin

How   when
Beverley Jacobs   stands up in Parliament
to speak of her grandmother's   'sexual beating'
demand respect   for First Nations women
and accept   a National Apology
how   not
to recall that night in Regina   how not to remonstrate with yourself
when the son of family friends   for remembering names of
got hammered on Jack with his buddy   the lawyer
drove to the North End   who argued for manslaughter
picked up a young woman   the mother
took her out to a field   who never stopped loving her son
for a blow job   the father
then beat her to death   who later took his own life
and left her there   but not

the name of the murdered Aboriginal woman?

How show respect   to a young woman
who helped her father   quit drinking
went down to the Stroll   twice a month
to earn some extra cash   to help bring up her kids
a beautiful   young woman
who took care   with her make-up and hair
found face-down   in the mud
battered so badly   her coffin was closed at the funeral
considered by the courts   just another dead hooker—
her killers 'good boys   who do stupid things'
given six and a half years   got out in four?

how not to regret   your own fear
that day you walked into   the Native Friendship Centre
intent on teaching   kids to read
but confronted   with a cartoon mural
of a blonde policewoman   slumped in an alleyway
stars   spinning
a bottle of Labatt's   smashed over her head
walked out   without saying a word

how to rake over your own past   but not resurrect Regina's two solitudes?

How flying over
this soiled ocean
           of chequered fields
spilled bloodlines,
               to reconcile your growing
devotion
               to the possibilities of poems
with a real recognition
               of the stranglehold
your language imposes
               on indigenous throats?

How, opening   not to laugh
Tales from the Smokehouse   woman, unleashing
at Daphne Odjig's dream   full of penises?
her medicine bag   see your own life
How not to   raging dreams
random desires
               joggling about in that bag?

27

How not
    at last
       to resonate
          with the tuning fork
             of the Kisiskatchewani Sipi
                  that deep green cleft
                      where your childhood still
                    flows between slopes
                of milkweed and sage
              flaming lilies
             and wild berries . . .
          snow-white, don't touch
          purple for pies . . .
        memories stirring
        like awakening birds
        in the thicket of your ribs
       as the swift currents below
      sing *welcome home*
      and the marzipan bomblet
     of a misâskwatômina
    explodes on your tongue
    like a nearly-familiar word
  it's not too late
  to learn

Tekahionwake

after E. Pauline Johnson
(1861–1913)

Canada's 'buckskin princess',
you criss-crossed your stolen country,
in rude new towns and cities
gathering, giving back
its shucked and scattered histories
of stoic chiefs, brave maidens,
and the battle of Cut Knife Creek.

For years your tragic ballads
entertained the crowds.
The night you spoke in Mohawk
they booed you off the stage.

༚

Your father, Onwanonsyshon,
counted as a friend
Sir Alexander Graham Bell.

When they tested the first telephone
from your family home, jokes
in Kanien'kehá:ka crackled across the call:

though history seeks to drain it,
the river of a language
can force a course uphill.

On The Day I Heard You'd Died

I was at home, checking work emails
after a weekend jolly in London.
Three were from a Palestinian poet
to whom I'd sent some thoughts
about poetry, war and martyrdom,
plus a poem in the voice of a jaded young Brit
encountering a photo of the severed head
of a teenage female suicide bomber.
In the first email the poet was so angry
he had deleted most of his initial response,
telling me only that my poem
"performed necropolitics" and "the failure
of empathy should never be used as a prop—
you ought to know better." In the second email
he apologised "for withdrawing," and attached
a dazzling poem about driving with his daughter
into a storm. In the third email he said
sorry again, that he'd been triggered
but I was not the source, and he wished
we could meet to discuss everything in person.
I wasn't sure if he was right about my poem, but
instantly knew that, yes, I should have known better
than to broach the subject of Palestinian violence
in an email with anyone, let alone him.
I felt stupid and sad. I replied, apologising
profusely, but pressed send too soon:
the next email I opened was a Word of the Day,
'incogitant', meaning 'thoughtless; inconsiderate',
which he probably would have liked, and
might have helped me get over the stupid feeling.
The next subject line was 'Confidential: Former Student.'
That was the email about you.
It didn't say how you'd died, but I'd taught you
poetry, and I didn't have to be told.
Oh Tori.
I liked your poems.

They were bleak and scary and witty:
I can still hear those wine bottles clanking,
still see that vacated flat with its white walls
and rotting apple core.
                    So why didn't I reply
to that Facebook message you sent about your first collection?
Because it was just a link to an Amazon page,
a self-publication notification with no salutation?
I could have said congratulations, at least.
Why didn't I do that?
Perform a simple act of kindness?
And why was I, right now, thinking about *me*,
as if anything I did or didn't do
had made one grain of difference to you?
I closed my laptop, grabbed my coat,
walked down to the beach and cried.
A small cry, vague and hopeless.
For you, with your Emergency Calls,
SOS social media posts,
and that little group of friends
who drifted in late, sat at the back, and disliked
so many of the poems in the textbook.
For the poems you did love, that fired your muse.
For your talent that will never mature.
And for me. For my failures and foolishness and vanity.
For my talent at performing necropolitics,
and stubborn reluctance to write honestly
about my own teenage suicide attempts.
For empty evenings and solitary summers.
For my libido, which has evaporated
like dew in the Sahara.
A small cry, whisked away on the wind,
like an injured kittiwake.
A cry that was also for Palestine,
that triggers me too, for good and ill;
for a girl in a refugee camp,

whose mother was a refugee and
whose grandmother was a refugee,
and who, rather than get married
and give birth to refugees
in her own country, left home
one morning wearing a bomb;
for the illusion of human communication,
with its gunpowder misunderstandings
that leave spreading grey stains on the heart.
For your father and his online outburst,
telling your friends to "get off Facebook
and get a life." For all young people
sucked into death cults
instead of being helped to live
with themselves, with each other
and death, which will find us all
soon enough. And finally,
with a hiccup and a pebble
hurled into the sea
as I get up to go home,
for the way tears dry,
grown-ups move on,
and the world keeps turning
its back on the people it breaks:
in Gaza, the West Bank,
Regina and Chichester
and littering the shorelines in between,
brittle star youths who will never learn
that eventually, if you write enough poems,
you can just about breathe into the pain.

True Patriot Love

after Joyce Wieland & Daphne Odjig

Oh, Canada.
My home and stolen land.
Yet again you've pulled
your woolly toque down
over the eyes of the world,
scored high as legal cannabis
on the International Peace Index,
and like a windblown hippie chick,
sucked back over the Atlantic
to demand her slice
of the placid national pie,
your prodigal adopted daughter
is strolling once more
your warm, wide streets,
soaking up the serenity
emanating from the tarmac
squeezed like miles
of grey toothpaste
across your uncomplaining soil.
For hey, what's there
to complain about
in the True North, stoned and free?
Here in Toronto, the cabbies
are eco-philosophers
solving the global biofuel crisis,
the hatmakers at artist co-ops
promote 'protective linen fibres,'
and judging from the corner stores
the whole city's blissed out
on herbal teas: aisles and aisles
of Tranquil Magic, Calming Karma,
Tension Tamer, Sleep EZ.
Even the thief
who nicks my brother's laptop,

iPod and prescription sunnies
is a model of courtesy,
a considerate criminal,
barely crossing the threshold,
kindly forgoing the TV and CDs,
while outside the apartment,
the gentle whoosh of street cars
passing through the night
whispers of the peace inherent
in transporting a tolerant,
multi-culti populace home
from the ball game,
the Leonard Cohen concert,
and the Liquor Board Store.
As the homeless man
at Spadina and College,
telling me jokes about yoghurt,
intuits, it's all quite
the "culture shock".
Oh Canada, how could I have
almost forgotten
your pregnant peace,
enormous as your four time-zones,
five Great Lakes,
numberless wildernesses
of cedar, birch and jack pine,
snowy plains and tundra,
mountain peaks and prairie dunes;
a peace that swarms
around me
like a humidity of midges;
a remote and swollen peace
ready to burst
like the millennia
of human thunder
still rumbling in the stony rim

of the Wanuskewin Sacred Hoop
         I visited near Saskatoon;
       and in my memory of that evening
          eighteen years ago,
            when, walking through
          Toronto's Christie Pits,
           and descending into
              the natural amphitheatre
         of its ancient creek bed,
       I felt the heartbeat of the land
              throbbing underfoot,
               drumming the song of a people
         who washed their children in a river
      long diverted into sewers,
         hunted deer in forests
      that became a gravel quarry
      worked by the tenants
           of the Shacklands,
        a clutter of hovels
       built for the shoeless Irish
     and runaway American slaves;
        cleared to create a civic park,
          the site, in 1933,
      of a bloody six-hour riot
     between a Jewish baseball team
    and a home-grown Swastika Club;
      and now a faded green hangout
       for lunching office workers,
         rough sleepers
            and drug dealers.
  Canada, that night I ached
           for your cities,
     for their misery and picnic tables,
          genocide and shady lanes,
       wished them smudged off the map
     by the smoky thumbprints

of global implosion,
a stick of burning sage;
for your granite shield to rise
against future incursions,
the survivors to mingle
bloodlines and traditions,
bison to once again
darken the plains.
Oh Canada, I was young,
just beginning to learn
what was mine to hate
and what mine to hold.
I wouldn't praise
your clean streets then,
or stitch your flag
onto my backpack.
Joyce Wieland's lipstick
scoring of your anthem,
her Xeroxed smooches
and flying pink penises,
were as embarrassing
as my mother's rows of x's
the bottom of her letters.
Letters I've just crossed
an ocean and a continent
to retrieve.
For in the generation since
that booming
summer's night,
Mum's death,
Joyce's blazing blue Arcadias,
Daphne's medicine
bag full of boners,
have taught me
we are here
to kiss the Earth.

So Canada, today,
as your headlines trumpet
a National Apology
to the Inuit, First Nations
and Métis
–though reconciliation
don't mean squit
  without reparation–
  just for now,
a balmy June afternoon
  in my forties,
  I'm all yours:
swinging down Queen St
  like a one-woman
    jazz fusion anthem,
Aboriginal hip hop
rising in my ear buds,
    my heart
a shimmering cymbal
    struck
by your broad brush
  of peace

2008–2018

Eva Gore-Booth and Con Markievicz
Gently Chide an Old Friend

The innocent and the beautiful
Have no enemy but time
*   —W.B. Yeats*

Beautiful? Maybe.
But innocent, Willie, we never were.
Beyond the great windows
how the ground rumbled—
the hoarse whispers of famine
we heard as girls
driving us away
from dreams of wild swans
and trailing kimonos,
into the march of crowds,
the hot arms of gunmen,
each in our own way
thunderous
for change.

Yes, a death sentence
unfairly deferred.
Yes, shadows growing
within a thin frame,
two not-yet-old faces
drawn in grey ink,
blanched by the light
that scours the air
between storms.

But time, sweet William,
was never the enemy:
time is the river
the dark cloud of desire
drinks and rains—
and though flower sellers cry,

circus girls sweat,
and visions of freedom
get wrung like red rags,
our hearts are cups
that catch every drop
and fling them
into the waves.

Ahed

It was the slap
that should have been heard
around the world. But the girl
– though fair-skinned, blonde,
her tawny mane an emblem
of her young lion's heart –
was not fighting for an education
or freedom from child marriage,
but for rights the world
had long ago decided did not fit
the grand plan for her land.
So the smack of her palm
on that soldier's cheek
was snatched by the wind
for a strictly limited whirl,
then locked up in a box
stamped: the sound
of one hand clapping.
And though the stripe marks
soon faded
and scratches healed,
a bruise on the chin
of a vulnerable prison state
is a serious matter;
the girl was tried
behind closed doors
in a military court
and, of course, locked up too:
the little slapper
who, with her blue eyes
and golden corkscrew curls
was clearly also guilty
of impersonating
the rightful owners
of her home –
an 'Insta-fada' fake,

cheap European import,
certainly no one
who might win
a Nobel Prize.

An Aisling

i.m. Flo Crawford

The wind's been high all day,
sweeping the clouds around the sky,
but the grave is rinsed by sunshine
as we peel away wet leaves,
tweak our bunch of flowers,
wipe the headstone clean.
You cross yourself, stand quietly;
I put my arm around you.
You're tinier than I remember,
walk more slowly now.
"I'm always afraid I'll snuffle,"
you say as we turn to go.

Now Toto chews her bone,
the electric coal fire burns,
and I'm getting you to talk
about the streets round here.
"Have you not heard of Máire Drumm?"
you ask, and you're away.

If Ian Paisley was Republican,
he would have been Máire Drumm:
she gave the fieriest speeches—
you could see the flames dance in her eyes.
Oh, the times she was arrested,
interned in Armagh Prison;
and when she was free
she baked cakes for the prisoners,
rallied women and children,
never missed a funeral or demo.
Máire was a good friend of Liam,
your sister Peggy's husband,
sure, you've mentioned him before.
It was Liam brought that film star—

yes, Vanessa Redgrave—
over to Belfast to talk about Palestine,
and when youse drove down to the Hall
youse were mobbed by photo-hunters.
Peggy met Liam at a party
after he got out of jail.
Twelve years, he was in,
apart from the time he escaped.
Oh, you remember that clearly,
your Mammy wouldn't let youse outside.
He and two other prisoners
dove into the Broadway Picture House;
Liam shouted "Free Ireland"
and gave a political speech.
On the street, the police started shooting,
killed a baby in a pram.

That was terrible sad,
but still it was rare round here.
The Lower Falls, yes, and Andersonstown,
but most people here didn't care
what religion anyone was.
Your own Granda was a Protestant,
and both your Daddy and Uncle George
joined the British Army.
Not because of England, mind,
there just wasn't any work.
George married a French girl,
but when she died in childbirth
he took a fierce Loyalist wife.
Your Mammy brought up Georgette
but even though George moved
to the slopes of Napoleon's Nose,
he never converted,
saying to the Mormons
that day on the doorstop,

"I may have lost my religion,
but I haven't lost my reason."

The Loyalist Wife would read your tea leaves,
but she never came down to the Falls.
You can't understand all that—
you and Peggy, Ann, Mona and Harry,
were never brought up to hate anyone.
Why, Protestants used to live round here:
it's their church became Cultúrlann.

So that story Mairtín told me,
about his aunty rattling dustbin lids?
Oh, that was just Ann:
three a.m. every ninth of August
she'd be out with all the neighbours
to commemorate the internment—
that day's the start
of the West Belfast Festival now.
No, if it wasn't for Derry and
the internment, the injustice of it all,
the bombers wouldn't have had the support;
but to round up Liam and put him in jail
just because the Queen
was drinking tea at Stormont—
well, we can giggle now,
but you can see why people fought back.

Still, your family was never political
and Liam never argued with youse.
He'd lost his own mother, and both his brothers—
Danny got caught in crossfire,
and when the other lad died,
Liam wasn't let out of jail.
No, Liam loved Mammy,
and she loved him,

and Mairtín made up his own mind.
Every weekend, you went to the library together.
And if he believed in a united Ireland,
that didn't make him sectarian:
look at Henry Joy McCracken,
a Protestant Republican,
hanged in 1798.

You get up to boil the kettle,
and I give the dog a cuddle.
Máire Drumm had an eye operation,
you'd said, and right in her bed
in the Mater Hospital
she was shot by Loyalists
dressed up as doctors—
even by Belfast standards,
that was beyond the pale.
There weren't any gunshots at Liam's grave,
but his casket was draped with a tricolour
and a piper played at the church.
Harry went young, the same year as your Daddy,
and when George followed,
his funeral parlour was lonely and cold:
none of his wife's people came.
Your Mammy passed away when Mairtín was small,
Peggy and Ann later on.
And last year, after taking a pilgrimage,
climbing hundreds of steps in the sun,
Mona collapsed in Croatia.
Fra brought her home in an air ambulance
and she died at City Hospital
without ever opening her eyes.
At least it wasn't the Royal Belfast,
where Mairtín was taken,
after you found him upstairs
on the floor in his room,
a bruise spreading over his forehead.

My hands are buried in Toto's fur;
you return with tea and biscuits,
ask if I'm warm enough.
You still get up in the morning,
make coffee for the home help,
go shopping for bargains—
new boots, a good coat;
you can still laugh, like today
when the clouds burst at last
and I lent you my scarf
to cover your head,
teasing "Now you're a real Irish woman."
You still read crime novels:
Every mother's worst nightmare.
Every year place a notice
to remember Mairtín:
"All God's gifts are good."

Máire Drumm blazed,
her tinderbox tongue
sparking the beacons of nation—
but you, Flo, gentle and grieving,
keep my dream of Ireland alive.
When we speak on the phone,
I'm right back in the streets
of a pearly grey city
embraced by distant green hills,
its black and white murals
and colourful kerbstones
washed clean
by a long winter rain.

Indelible

i.m. Razan al-Najjar

Her mother clutches the evidence—
a white coat no longer

white, but rust red, blotched,
like the hide of a gazelle

discarded by drunken poachers
after slaughtering the herd.

As cameras circle, newsfeeds buzz,
this woman's grief points like a finger

to a truth beyond proof:
its Red Crescent still

just visible, this vest
is mercy's banner, sunset-stained.

Shaking the Bottle

for Sunny Singh

My eighteenth birthday, at a well-naff restaurant,
Mum gave me a 'good luck penny':
a rind of copper jammed in an old Bolly cork.
"We drank the champagne for your christening, pet—
now this is to keep you afloat."

It was the kind of tat you lose
before you even sling your coat on.
I was only half-joking when I said
she should have saved me the bottle instead.

That day in Jerusalem, a girl my age
exploded at a bus stop. The bomb she had on
killed two Israeli soldiers, wounded sixteen people,
and blasted her body to steam. Her head,
still wrapped in its scarf, shot off in an arc down the street.

The pics that popped up in my inbox
were 'martyrdom posters' from a Palestinian kids' magazine:
the girl's head, smack dab on the pavement,
papped like a Halloween queen.

Those closed eyes: what did they see?
I googled, clicked and scrolled, found
bullets and bulldozers gouging out her streets,
soldiers, politicians, stamping down her dreams.

They say the future's ours to fizz up,
smash against their tanks. Hey, like, wicked. Thanks.
Suppose I could have talked to Zainab?
What would I have said? *Wake up girl,*
learn English, get on Myspace, join the plebs?

Once I stuffed a letter into one of Mum's blue bottles,
torched the paper with my lighter,
hurled the hot glass from the beach.
Just another bit of rubbish, bobbing out of reach.

The Book of Wives

But the queen Vashti refused to come at the king's commandment by his chamberlains: therefore was the king very wroth, and his anger burned in him.
    —The Book of Esther 1:12 (King James Version)

I. Vashti

Esther, the scholars have named books for you,
have called you the daughter of Ishtar,
Queen of the Morning Star.

Of me they have written that I would not dance
because my flesh was white with leper's flakes,
or I had sprouted a demon's tail.

My skin is cracked leather now,
my face a bitter walnut,
my hands flecked with spots of mould.

But I am alive. I wake to bird song
and first light. Drink clear water
from a blue flagon. Eat tooth-splitting village bread.

For though he told the world his lions had devoured me,
Xerxes could always be persuaded . . .
and thus I am still pacing in my hut.

The eunuchs bring me fruit,
bruised wives leave honey cake on the step,
and the odd, myopic peacock struts into my trap.

Esther, though—Esther in your royal robes,
you have never visited. But you know
I am here, and that it is to me you owe

the blood on the lips of your people.
The glossy scarlet blood
that clots your mouth shut

whenever our husband curses your fame,
seeks to cleanse his soiled pride
in the pool of my disgrace.

II. Esther

Some, I know, whisper
I am no heroine:

should have stood in sisterhood,
declined to take your place;

should have spoken sooner
to reveal Jewish blood.

But it was your fate, Vashti,
that showed me

none can refuse
the commands of a king.

And though rumour has it
he keeps you like a collared dove

in a mud hut in the desert,
your hold on his soul

teaches me only that it takes time
to turn oak into poplar,

and like a warm wind by the river,
bend a man's will to your own.

III. Vashti

Esther, little sister,
you inherited my banquet hall:
its gold and silver curtains
lustrous purple hangings

still tremble with the echoes of my refusal
to strip between its marble pillars
and dance a whore's dance for my King.

The eunuchs shuffled fatly at the door,
scrutinized their jewelled belts.
The wives of foreign princes
hid their titters behind ivory fans—

I watched their sooty lashes
bat secret messages of delight
across my laden table. And where once
my heart beat only for him
and the touch of his hot fingers,
now, deep in our desert palace, it froze
like a howling chunk of mountain
no man would ever summit again.

Some mornings I sluice my naked body
with the ice melt of that fury—
then my nipples glint like spear tips,
and my cold heels stamp his face into the mud.

You, though, shelter in the shadow
of the date palm he planted
on our wedding day,
and now half-cocks his leg to piss on

like a wounded dog.

IV. Esther

After thirty days
of absence from his bed,

it took three days of fasting
to summon the courage

to seek an audience
with my husband,

risk the fatal lowering
of his golden sceptre.

When Xerxes smiled instead,
bid me enter his chamber,

it took two nights
of feasting and wine

to simmer his heart
in the warm oil of my beauty,

infuse my humble pleading
with the scent of sesame and thyme—

and thus save my uncle
from Haman's gallows,

my people
from the sword.

And though I know, Vashti,
it is in your jealous nature

to ever seek the last word,
in treading soft and slow

I raised my name above yours
to a festival in the heavens—

a promise of deliverance
that shines down all the years.

V. Vashti

O Esther, purest sister,
he still comes,
tail between his legs

to slobber his apologies,
paw my withered breasts.
But this much I will grant you:

though your birth name
means myrtle,
you are no shy starry flower.

When you rewrote your King's decree,
allowed the Jews to kill
all who might attack them,

you burned your name
into the human night
with a knife of blinding light.

Nestless

for Mordechai

Is a bird still a bird
    without wings or song?
Ask the Whistle Blower—
feathers clipped
    beak bound with barbed wire
    he stalks the streets
of a riven city
tracks the scars across its hills
    scents the wind
    awaits the call

His heart's a booming bittern
    trapped in a prophet's tomb
the lightning in his eye
    a silent eagle's shriek
the telling of his secret peace
    vanunu vanunu vanunu
a downy coo
    that wears away all walls

The Purse

for Dareen Tatour & Einat Weizman

It arrived in a Jiffy bag, my reward
for supporting *Prisoners of the Occupation*, a play
by an Israeli woman, banned and denounced
by the Minister of Culture, vilified online
for 'glorifying terrorists', terrorists
like the young woman who'd embroidered
twenty-eight purses for the crowdfunding campaign
while under house arrest
for writing a poem.

It was larger than I'd expected, a flat purse
with a metal lip and clasp, covered in black cloth
and row upon row of red circles and green crosses,
interlocking flowers and wheels, the kind of pattern
the eye just can't stop making new sense of,
simple but complex, molecular, celestial, iconic,
and so comfortable in my palm holding it
was like shaking the capable hand of its maker.

The next day I woke up early, into a stretch of time
I wouldn't normally enjoy; a time for counting blessings.
Starting with sixty tiny green crosses of two stitches each;
fifty-six large green crosses of ten stitches each;
two hundred and twenty red petals, twenty-four stitches each;
and fifty-six red rings of sixteen stitches each.
A total of—I had to get my calculator out—
six thousand eight hundred and fifty-six stitches.

At, let's say, ten seconds a stitch, that's
sixty-eight thousand five hundred and sixty seconds,
or just over nineteen hours. Allowing a minute
every two hundred stitches for rethreading and knotting,
and ten minutes an hour for tea-making and sipping,
adds another one hundred and ninety-five minutes,
for a total of twenty-two hours and fifteen minutes,
or just under a long sleepless day of Dareen's life,
of which she has, so far, including the leap year,
spent one thousand and two days locked up,
waiting for court dates, reading Darwish,
praying, laughing, and sewing purses
full of poems.

July 9th 2018

The Dead Sea

for Munzer

No host of minnows
swarmed over me.
No five-fingered weed
grasped my ankle,
sucked me down
to a bed
of black mud.
Suspended
in a shrinking soup
of water, salt
and skin,
I drifted
alone and star-splayed,
as far beneath the sun
as a distant day
can plunge—
here, in the
lifeless heart
of a plundered land,
you gave me
the fugitive warmth
of the womb.

A Monoglot Proofreads Arabic

As I adjust the fonts and spacing, correct
mirrored diacritics, use pattern recognition
to spot egregious typos, find homes for orphaned lines,
I suppose my dedication might seem odd:
a misplaced semicolon in the holy book of love,
clasping sentences that ought to stand apart.
But cut and pasting perky camels, little hats,
jasmine ovules and feluccas, I understand this script,
with its inky incense tendrils, is tattooing and lassoing me
into its fragrant depths—a fate I quietly embrace;
for sometimes when I paint brown lines around my eyes,
draw a crimson bow for the arrow of my tongue,
it seems I've spent my life in service
of a language I can neither read nor speak.

Not there yet

Much as I wish to write only poems
in which tall trees stand
for the lungs of the world and the moon
rises like a sigh in their branches,
I still sometimes dream
of being a serial killer. Tonight
I raped a faceless young woman
in a corrugated sewage tunnel,
disembowelled her and smeared
fistfuls of viscera and shit
over the tender breasts
of my trembling
accomplice, an act I filmed
and stored on a micro-SD card
soon discovered
by the IT guy sent to fix my work
computer, a silent man I hunted in the dark
playing fields of a secret NATO base,
awakening at four a.m.
just before the slaughter. To heal
the disappointment,
I watched YouTube videos
of Arab poets honouring
the bougainvillea, refusing,
in voices like mountains
of dark sugar,
to let their sons become soldiers.
Outside, the moon
coldly sings another body's song
and the bare elms
continue, unperturbed,
their long slow exhalation
into spring.

Adamantine

for Elisabeth Fritzl

Chained in the cellar
until the chain interfered
 with his pleasure,
rats your only company,
 water flooding down the walls,
you were bone cold all winter,
 sweltered through the summers
as your family splashed
 in the swimming pool above you—
an alibi luxury, built to explain
the earth your filthy burrow
 had displaced. Down there,
     to punish you
  for the tiniest defiance
he plunged you into darkness
     for days on end,
         the only light
shed by the brutal porn
 he made you re-enact.
He barely ever spoke,
 delivered your seven babies
  with dirty scissors
   and disinfectant;
 incinerated one, took three
 upstairs, to believe
you'd abandoned them;
 left three with you
   in that sunless hole,
grey-skinned ghosts
 with rotting teeth,
forced to grow up watching,
 over and over again,
a wolf with their own features
devouring their mother.
 I don't know how you did it,

but Elisabeth, you survived.
  Didn't starve yourself to death.
Didn't smash your brains out.
  Didn't do to your children
    what he did to you.
Your father chose you "for his own"
  because you were uncontrollable—
a truant with a lip on her,
  a climbing rose he couldn't train.
But you were always
    your own lodestone,
    a glinting adamant
hidden, growing, drilling
    through the walls
of that other buried cell:
the dug out air-raid shelter
  his mother forced him
    down into alone
  when the bombs began to fall.

The Facts

it was no longer possible
to live with them all
some had to be shrink-wrapped
others ground to powder   or returned
in a spring epiphany of upward rain
yet somehow   tongueless nightingales
and child brides remained

stumbling on an answer   educating girls
I arrived back   where I started
to feel again   the open space
around me   in the world

Mama Africa

for Colin Grant & Jo Alderson

back of the blues tent
festival midnight
too cold for beer
summer rain in my hair
Bessie, Billie
Amy, Millie
swim through a new throat
until Gizzelle bids farewell
to sorrow & stage lights
her sweat-soaked gardenia
neon tattoos
bopping out to the beat
of a classic ska encore
& interval chitchat
lollipops from Jamaica
to Regina, Saskatchewan
'round about eighty-four
that Peter Tosh concert
at the Centre for the Arts
what was he like?
Can't remember a note
just the skinny hash joint
Randy rolled in the Chev
and the fifty Rizla spliff
big as a dij
Tosh lit up on stage
to the sigh of the crowd
if we weren't high before
we were now, we were now
but if the memories
don't flood back
you gotta slow-reel 'em in
and if the line floats by . . .
my muscles were shivering?

he wore obsidian shades?
you gotta
weigh it down
way down
there
where
a dangerous bass riff
throbs up from the pit
of a plush theatre seat
slyly bonds with my spine
my blown open
young mind
in a Boeing boing bong
that stretches me long
drubs me like dough
moon rooms me
soon come
boomtowns me
warm throng
doom thumps me
dumbfoundling
loom hangs me low
deep in some womb fume
where the randoms
don't go
each thick string
a slick thong
thrumming
you belong
you belong
sixteen-year-old
white girl
you belong
you belong
before Bunny
before Bob

before Dub
before boys
and their hip guns
before falling in love
bang bang
summer's hum
before your small ears
were formed
the first reverb
you ever heard
was your mother's
bass drum
& her mother's
bass drum
& her mother's
bass drum . . .

Bessie n Billie
Billie n Millie
Amy n me
me n me
the first reverb
the world heard
was our black mothers'
bass drum

Winterpause

The hours since I saw you last
Have left me in an unknown past
  —Nico

Trees. Graffiti. Windows. Dirt and snow.
The Ringbahn and its sun-bleached views
of brickworks, *Garten Hausen,* empty lots,
a punkette with two German Shepherd bitches.

Scab of dereliction, taut and satiny beneath
its tender crust of blood and yellow stars—Berlin
is where the young desire the old. *Aber nicht*
nur für die Kinde: Techno DJs, druggy witches,

puppet operas, the grainy, backlit gloss
of *Weihnachten* wooden toys. Hedgehogs
scratch and scuffle past the stairwells of the East;
wild boars on the outskirts snuffle in the ditches.

Is it city, forest, or your songline, Christa Päffgen,
I step through to your grave?

<p

Nico Icon? No. In my mirror, *Image Mage*—
The Factory, your famous fucks, scleral pinprick gaze,
barely etched the surface of your power:

now you, who alchemised a man's name, milked
a glassy vision from the grimy marble years,
are reunited with your mother in a pine and ivy bower.

On the black shock of your headstone, a banana
darkly ripens like my smile. Above, in snowy needles
a sallow little bird flutters like a flower.

A transmigrating voice, I follow flight paths to no ends.
You, a deeper voyage, droning bowl of fruitless dreams,
lament no more the lateness of the hour.

I photograph the silence of a white sky bruised with gold—
the winter sun has won her foggy struggle with the cold.

Left to My Own Devices

My Dell laptop with its airplane engine fan and sticky number four key.
The fifteen kilo Lynx tablet the university bought me for conferences
that, like my sulky ex, finds my work so dull it goes to sleep
and locks if I don't continually caress it during my presentations.
The touch insensitive BlackBerry PlayBook that, unlike my ex,
will occasionally respond to indignant jabs and screams of fury.
The suspect motherboard replaced by the blonde Polish engineer
and the one she installed, that failed to solve the black screen issue
on my second brand-new all-in-one Dell desktop in a month.
The timid all-in-one before that, which froze while browsing,
and the anxious one that crinkled empty crisp packets all day long.
My retro Kindle Classic that, by diktat of its Amazon overlords,
refuses downloads, demanding cut, paste and email ops instead.
My BlackBerry handset that greets efforts to search the internet
with an 'expired server certificate chain' error message
no O2 Guru the length and breadth of Britain
knows how to eliminate . . .
pulverise them all
let
a
pair
of monstrous jaws
chew 'em up, spew out a whispering cascade
of plastic, copper, steel and rare earths microbeads,
black flecks, metallic glints of the invisible negativities
that underwrite our universe. Into this granular antimatter
sprinkle handfuls of every shoreline I've ever staked a towel on
from Thailand's fine white sand and the olive leaf litter of Paxos,
the dun earth of Regina Beach and mineral grit of the Dead Sea,
to a powdery blend of Brighton pebbles, shells and broken bottles;
add a pinch of candlelight, crushed mountain peak and lark song,
then stir the coruscating swirl into an hour glass just my height
and hoist it on a spider's thread into the void inside my head
so, like an agoraphobic member of the Dark Skies Society,
on pilgrimage in a diamond mine, a patient in a recovery clinic
for anthropocene diseases, I may remember how to measure time
in long slow revolutions, scintillating rivers, the ceaseless flow
of subtle light and tantalizing toxins through my vast interior,
the magnetic heart and guts and flux of the whole insoluble world.

Saint Mildew and the Druggan

Far from fair, and round about,
upon a furry, fangled night,
Saint Mildew had just snuffed her snout
when who should hone her hoary light?

Say not so, and say it surly,
squash the clocks and praise the poor,
but sure as Frangipan's a girlie,
a Druggan scritchled at the door.

A Druggan? No! A *Druggan*? Yes!
She heard the smirk; she smelled the hiss.
Saint Mildew starched her starkest dress,
from mangrove mirrors milked a kiss.

For when a Druggan comes a-corbling,
drag not thy heels in mercy's mire.
Stiff like Mildew, lift thy stingwing,
shade thine eyegaze from the fire.

Just one squint at that torn face
will desecrate both Love and Hate—
an empty light shall fill the place
where once the heart did resonate:

tender feelings shrink to pinpricks,
courage, passion burn to black,
the Druggan's cold and ghostly flame licks
clean the platter, slick the lack.

Silver pencils poked through keyholes,
windows shone like glockenspiels—
Mildew called on nineteen foe-souls:
"Winch me up on war-sawn wheels!"

As that soaring, whirring fury
split the door from North to South,
blindly seeking hymnal glory
she launched a spear-shot from her mouth.

The Druggan reared, the Druggan roared,
its throat as snaky as a swan's.
From that face dark splendour poured:
the Druggan shone like phosphor bronze . . . .

But though with pure and piercing verse
Mildew skewerskilled the beast,
naught could salve her light-scorched voice,
not virgin's tears nor tongue of priest.

Now she drones the ancient songs,
her toothless Truthless Beauty brings
a monotone of rites and wrongs
to homeless bones and tarnished rings.

Going on Crutches to Grenfell Tower

If you want to see how the poor die, come see Grenfell Tower.
    —Ben Okri

A Nigerian summons me to London from the sea.
A Palestinian gives me directions from the south bank of the river.
As I hesitate at the head of a plummeting escalator
two sharp-suited businessmen turn to help me
descend into the Underground.
It's rush hour and the carriages are crammed.
I shrug off my backpack,
tuck it with the crutches close to my body,
and reach for the overhead rail, realising too late
all this is difficult, strains my weak arm—
as the force of the train rocks through me,
an Irishman asks if I need any help.
"I'm okay", I say, and lurch against the door.
Quietly, in an almost formal gesture
that reminds me of the way
South Koreans offer money,
he grips my elbow, holds my arm
between Waterloo and Westminster—
to keep him upright, he laughs
before he hops off
and I squeeze into his place by the plexiglass partition
with its blessedly vertical grab-rail.
"Will someone give this lady a seat?"
another man asks. Not a single person looks up.
Only one of my fellow passengers is asleep.
"Charming," I murmur. The man repeats his question
and a woman stands, without a word or a glance.
I sit. I have taken her seat,
her prized rush hour seat,
but I needed to sit.
I felt unsafe on my feet.

 ℘

If you want to see how the poor die, come see Grenfell Tower.
At Baker St it strikes me
that heeding the call of the poet
wasn't, perhaps, such a great idea.
As I teeter down a flight of stairs
a train arrives at the platform below,
and a flood of humanity rises toward me,
filling the stairwell, a solid mass,
I can't thread my way through or bypass.
Neither can I turn around and go back.
I have to wait on the step
as people push past me.
I feel guilty for waiting.
For taking up space. For taking up time.
I feel stupid for thinking I could cross London on crutches.
I shouldn't have come.
I'm no Biblical cripple
journeying to Christ.
I don't need to be another Grenfell gawker.
I need step-free access
to a train home to Brighton.
But just as I realise
how foolish I've been, I see
that a small miracle is occurring:
people have noticed me,
are pressing closer together,
and a path has appeared,
a narrow, shining hemline
along the edge of the stairs:
an invitation to continue.
Hugging the wall, I step
down to the platform
as the physiotherapist taught me:
"Good foot to heaven,
bad foot to hell."

☙

On the Circle line, a petite black woman
smiles, jumps up, insists I sit,
and tells me about her corrected fourth toe.
She disembarks at Royal Oak,
and a tall, ruddy-cheeked couple gets on—
the woman looks at my black Formfit boot,
laughs a big, Midwest American laugh,
and asks "How long do you have to go?" . . .
and before I know it, the train isn't underground anymore,
we are rushing over grey streets and grey parks
and council estates, beneath a dull white sky,
then we are there, at Latimer Road,
and before the train has even pulled into the station
it is there too. Right there,
through the window, watching us
with its hundreds of burnt-out eyes.
Watching us go on with our lives.
Will we speed through its shadow?
Or step into its radius . . .
enter a crime scene
come home to a war zone
or make an unsteady pilgrimage
to a place we would normally zoom past?

If you want to see how the poor die, come see Grenfell Tower.
They greet me at the turnstiles.
Their faces are everywhere.
From walls, church railings, shop windows, telephone kiosks,
above the stiff queues of flowers,
the perfume of stargazers and rot,
their beauty radiates: an intolerable heat.
The curly-haired girl, on the cusp of her womanhood.
The honey-skinned mother and her five-year-old daughter.
The Muslim couple and their baby.
The two young Italians.
Women in bright sweaters, bold prints, smiles and hijabs.

Older men clad in dignified solitude.
Steven, also known as Steve.
Mohammed from Syria . . . *please sign the petition.*
Poster after poster, *please call . . .*
if you see . . .
And behind the telephone kiosk,
that plastered pillar of love,
with its poems and prayer calls
and white paper butterflies,
behind the viaduct
with its incessant trains,
behind the vinyl banner
on the brick-clad new build—
'Considerate Constructors
Secure Everyone's Safety':
it rises.
The blackness
I have hobbled here
to stare at
as if nothing else exists.
The blackness
I will never forget.
For there is nothing blacker
than the windows
of Grenfell Tower.
Not the *niqab* of the young woman
at the zebra crossing
whose dark darting eyes
are the essence of light,
not the black plastic boot
that protects my shattered ankle,
not the black shell of my laptop
on which I'm writing this poem,
or the fascia of my BlackBerry phone
on which I took grainy photos
of the burnt-out windows

of Grenfell Tower,
photos that fail
to show those windows
as they are:
blackness as void.
The unfathomable blackness
we come from and return to.
Absolute blackness.
Cordoned off by red and white ribbons,
guarded from gawpers
by police in florescent jackets,
but impossible to cover up,
impossible to hide,
yet impossible to approach,
until a man strides by me,
stops up ahead on the pavement
and raises his arms.
Pale, grey-haired, in a grey shirt,
his arms lifted to the Tower
in an open-palmed V
for veneration,
he appears to be praying,
mourning, giving healing,
sending love to Grenfell Tower,
communing with the spirits,
he tells me,
of his neighbours
who went to school with his children,
who *didn't want to leave this way—*
whose agony lodges in his throat,
whose vanished beauty shines in his eyes
as he turns to go back home.

If you want to see how the poor die, come see Grenfell Tower.
Yes, Grenfell Tower is a mass grave,
a mausoleum, a crematorium.
It commands our silence.
But go and see it.
Go and see Britain's black omphalos,
the navel of our failure
to take care of each other.
Go and see London's real Olympic Torch,
our monument to everything this country's leaders do best:
scoffing at basic safety procedures, flouting regulations
—flouting the very *concept* of regulations—
ignoring expert advice, ridiculing experts,
cutting corners, padding bank accounts,
promising improvements, delivering death traps,
telling critics to 'get stuffed',
never consulting, never respecting
the people they are paid to represent:
people deemed a nuisance and an eyesore,
a blight on property values,
a threat to 'social order',
whose lives are not worth the paper
their missing posters are printed on,
whose inevitable incineration
has been planned, approved and fully costed,
whose raw, homeless hearts
must be micromanaged
with a drip feed of numbers,
a narrowing of remits,
a stealthy adjournment of truth.
Yes, go see Grenfell Tower.
Go by tube, bus, car, taxi, bicycle,
wheelchair, skateboard, roller blades,
tap the pavement with white canes, with crutches.
Go and see it. Don't take a selfie.
Take flowers, food and clothes.

Leave a message at St Clements.
Go and see Kensington's anti-Kaaba,
its site of sacred devastation
rising in every direction we face.
And if you cannot go,
wherever you may be, however frail or far,
stand with the disappeared
and the survivors,
let us stand with the uncounted,
the discounted,
at the top of the stairs
on the twenty-fourth floor,
let us demand those responsible
for this preventable inferno
stop their frantic climbing
over Grenfell's missing bodies,
Grenfell's weeping firefighters,
Grenfell's tower of ashes,
to a well-insulated freedom
they do not deserve.
As faces fade
and memory flickers,
by the candles of our witness
let us light
a clear broad path
to justice on the street.
With its hundreds of burnt-out eyes,
from behind its clean white veil,
Grenfell Tower is watching us.
We cannot fail again.

June 2017–Nov 2018

THE CANCER BREAKTHROUGH

After the Biopsy

An iron pea
        in a skinned pillow,

mushrooming marble
        in a sack of aspic,

trespasser acorn
        sprouting in flesh—

yet, strangely, it doesn't feel
        strange to be hosting

this small numb planet,
        possible death star,

this bullet embedded
        in a clutch of blubber,

suspended
        a shade from my heart.

What my fingers have found
        is the nub
of my days here on Earth—

a dark maternal pearl
        secreted

by my oyster breast.

Diagnosis

The ultrasound room is dark and cool.
The radiologist smears gel on her wand,
squints at a black and white blur.
"What have they told you?" she asks.

I just know I've flown home early from Prague,
unseasonable storms over Europe
and a hole in Gatwick's main runway
sucking me into a vortex of delays and cancellations,
a heart-hammering race across Frankfurt airport,
and a nauseous night bus
from Heathrow to Brighton,
because the breast-care clinic insists
on giving me my diagnosis early,
plus another lymph node biopsy
as the first didn't yield a result—

the doctor keeps mum,
clicks her big needle
into my pathological armpit, leaves me
sticky and bruising beneath a paper sheet,
a chill sliding over my skin.

"Breast cancer's the new flu!"
the Polish nurse says as I dress,
then confides: "But your lump is round.
It looks benign to me."

My breast lump is round.

Despite all I know:
my mother died of colon cancer
at the age of fifty-two;
I'm forty-nine,
and consider the national alcohol limits
a sexist conspiracy against women writers,

exercise a stroll to the wine shop;
I've been summoned home
from a cushy teaching post
for a consultation with a breast cancer surgeon;
two plus two equals four—
I float upstairs on a June breeze

to be told I have a fast-growing, invasive ductal carcinoma,
Grade 3, four centimetres, Oestrogen and HER2-positive,
and will require a mastectomy;
six cycles of chemotherapy; ten years of Tamoxifen;
a lymph node clearance that could cause
a painful, incurable swelling of the arm;
and, as soon as possible, CT and MRI scans
to determine if the cancer has spread
to my liver or lungs.

"You were so calm,"
Lee says in the hall.
But I only sounded calm.
I was a frozen flower,
a white-lipped daisy, lost
in the freak summer avalanche
of all I should have known.

After the Consultation

Gripped by black tongs,
chained to a beam,
hoisted by men masked
against spatter and steam—

a crucible of furnaced bronze
pours into the cast of a breast
a woman must lose at all cost:
beneath her pale dress

the nibbled rose
of an aging nymph
sheds wormy clumps
into a river of lymph.

The foundry is a deafened opera,
an incandescent stage.
I watch, agog,
from the Gods,

hollow and tuned
to a silent act of treason,
vitrified by the grand finale
of my heedless season:

stripped to a porcelain corset,
hammered by fear
and blasted by facts,
a dog-whistle soprano spits and cracks—

arcs of garnet sparks,
nodes and nerves and ducts
spurting from her fissured shell
into the gasp of the stalls.

As if tip-toeing over my skin,
the surgeons emerge from the wings—
their sterile steel
not quite outshone

by the forgers' nippled gong.

MRI

Midnight thunder
at the breast bone,
a fist on a lover's locked door

I pretend not to hear—
try instead to breathe deep, sleep,
and prepare for the nurse's next call,

for my torso to flood
with absolute cold
at the sound of her voice,

until my guts are a scrim
of liverish ice
that takes all I've got

to warm and disperse
with the faltering flame
of blue calm—

this, not the scans,
the samples and needles
of blood, nodes and cells,

is the test.

Waiting for the Liver Scan Results

One, Two, Three, Four . . .
the stage is unnumbered thus far,
but invisible hands
have spike-marked the floor,

outlined in shiny white tape
a sofa, a table, a bed,
a toilet, a sick bowl.
On the proscenium, facing the seats,

she stands at a window frame
and rehearses her soliloquy on death.
Words, each a taut globe, burst
like rare grapes in her mouth

until she's skinned her own flesh
and swallowed the pips.
Light shrinks; a corvid squawks.
Its silhouette feathers a plywood front door.

Out in the dark, a stage hand claps,
the director taps notes,
and in the last row—a glint of specs—
the writer deletes the rest of the script.

ℒ

One for sorrow, two for joy . . .
but in South Korea a magpie means good luck.
Off book at last, she steps from the stage
into an English garden, fragrant with rain.

Unnoticed, another door, open a crack,
slowly recedes on invisible tracks—
not quite disappearing as the curtain falls
on the glistening bones of the opening act.

Aubade

no birds
no iPod genius mix
just the hum
of the extractor fan
the gleam of a tap
and the gentle parting of fingers
combing for hair
long dark spirals suspended
in water, stranded
like those on my pillowcase
abandoning my scalp
floating free
of this wakeful dream
until I gather and lift them
to the rim of the bath
array a fine etching
of unravelling nests, chased
by a fleet, chemic moon . . .
under this spell
I am unrecognisable
Ophelia in the stream
trailing frail pondweed
the Lady of Shalott
weaving poisoned locks
into half-sick lovers' knots
as water drips
cells shrink
a soapy mirror melts
and crowning my lost night
the force of a skull
seeks the touch
of light

Rough Justice

The UK lifetime cancer risk rate is now 1 in 2.

Everybody has cancer. Abnormality lurks
in the renaissance walls of our cells.
Chemo's the new mercury: metallic assassin, it works

its sizzling way through our veins, stripping perks,
searing nerves, scorching hair, hissing as it kills:
Everybody has cancer . . . abnormality lurks

in the twist of a helix, an innocent cough, the quirks
of a habit some wear well, to others spells:
chemo's the new mercury—metallic assassin, it works

to a contract signed at birth, a fleet of scarlet Mercs
sharking through intimate tunnels, pillowy hills.
Everybody has cancer. Abnormality lurks

like obscene graffiti, Hyena God circle jerks,
in our breasts, our brains, our souls' dark wells.
Chemo's the new mercury—metallic assassin, it works

like Casanova's quicksilver, scalding his irk-
some eleven infections, a long dose of fresh hells.
Everybody has cancer: abnormality works.
Chemo's the new mercury. Metallic assassin. It lurks.

Western Intervention

A soft pop. The power button light goes out.
No red, no green, just a soot-black screen—
right when I need to watch the fucking thing.
Comedies, nature docs, *Bake Off*, Van Gogh on Catch Up:
that's what the nurse said. Strictly no news. No barking Brexiteers, no
racist killer cops, no terrorist attacks in France or Iraq, and absolutely no
Syria. No blood-soaked children, no bunker bombs or white phosphorus, no
famished civilians, no shattered ceasefires, no shelled aid convoys, no
cratered hospitals, no babies dug from the rubble, tiny rigid
corpses buried in tea towels as activists cry
Where is everyone?

I'm under doc's orders: screen all that out, hook up to a feel-good IV.
Penny drops me off at the shop. The replacement Samsung
is a twenty-two-inch spanner in my plans to walk to City Hall—
but the box isn't so heavy, the September sun mild.
I shuffle through town, lodge my Housing Benefit appeal, sit
sipping water, shiver in the shade, text Olga for a lift, watch
yoga mums, eco-hipsters, Corbynistas traipse by
as above us all, vapour trails erase the blue, last gasp
holiday-makers heading from Gatwick to Greece. *How lucky
I am to be here*, I think yet again.

The midnight sky over A&E is a moonless mesh
of cloud and exhaust. *Sharp scratch*, a nurse warns.
Machines bleep. Numbers flash. Liquids drip. Western medicine
doing what it does: carpet bombing my body, killing to cure.

Aleppo, I breathe to the blazing hall light, *I'm watching*.
But I'm broken. I've got cancer, no savings, not enough sick pay
or blood in my veins—nothing to give, nothing to share
except a burning, hungry, million-star-strong will to live.

If It Is a War . . .

for Sara 'FizzySnood' Cutting

The war on cancer is fought in furtive exchanges
of stained rayon frocks, loud ties, frayed leather belts,
left against orders in plastic bags at the doors of closed shops,
steam-cleaned in back rooms, tagged and hung
by immigrants, retirees, transwomen and students,
fingered by party girls, single mums, lads between jobs,
worn-out lecturers on zero-hour contracts
who don't earn enough to Gift Aid.

The war on cancer is waged by athletic baristas,
weekend cyclists, half-marathon runners, hill climbers,
cake-bakers, crochet vest-makers; their media queen
a beaming bald veteran, posting bad jokes and fab pix:
a kooky carousel of tiaras, tinsel and fruit fascinators
crowning her stubble, she commands: *dig deep,
past the shrapnel for a fiver, a tenner—
#NowGoCheckYourBits!*

Armies of lab rats bite not-magic bullets;
generals clink champagne flutes at celebrity dinners—
but from control rooms to trenches, everyone knows
the war on cancer will be won by the dead:
their anonymous names engraved on brass plaques
screwed to ice-cap machines and hospital walls,
commemorating lumps with lump sums,
in thanks, in memory, in hope for us all.

The Cancer Breakthrough

Will not take place in a lab
or corporate boardroom;
won't foam in a test-tube,
blink in code on a screen,
be hawked for mega-bucks
by big pharma,
or flood the world's RSS feeds.

The cancer breakthrough
is happening now
and again, and again—
in the echoing space,
that cold ocean of years,
between one heart
and another.

Don't Count Your Lumpectomies

i.m. Eva Saulitis

Then, like a rainbow
floating in an oil spill,
it comes—

good news.

The "Oh. You mean I won't be an Amazon after all?" announcement;
the this-is-why-women-marched-in-the-streets-for-Herceptin update;
the go gladden your aunt, hearten your father, tell all your friends,
"The marathon's just begun, but I'm streaks ahead of the pack!"

revelation

that my pre-surgery chemo four MRI scan
shows no sign of disease in the breast.

It's the miracle I didn't dare ask people to pray for;
the vindication of my transformation
into a fasting, juicing, blogging, almost jogging, trampoline-ing nun;
the "I did it! I vanished the fucker!"
cascading gold fortune
I share one bitten coin at a time.

Because the result's unofficial, must be confirmed
by tissue samples after the lymph clearance,
reinforced by a month of radiotherapy,
a decade of hormone blockers
and a year more of that bloody big Herceptin needle
no one mentioned before.
Because my armpit is sore,
and the place where the tumour was itches.
Because my white blood cell count is so low
chemo six was postponed a week
delaying surgery until I don't know when

and if I have to post two major updates
on social media this month
I'll spend my whole life
sending cat stickers and smiley faces
instead of writing novels and poems.

I want to make people happy.
I want to be happy.
I know nothing is real
until it's on Facebook.
But I'm so tired I can't even go to bed:
just looking at pyjamas exhausts me.
Despite the best efforts of the volunteers
my wings are still slicked to my ribs
and, unlike cancer tumours,
rainbows are renowned for disappearing.

The Horses of Hvolsvöllur

For years she imagined flesh craters, a red raw moon burned into a chest. Then she saw photographs of a radical mastectomy: smooth skin meeting like lashless eyelids along the seams of two elegant white scars, and later on this woman's beauty helped cushion the shock of her diagnosis. She was grateful for all of the cushions. The nurse gave her two made by hospital volunteers, heart-shaped ones, to tuck under her arm after surgery; the partially-blind sculptor she'd met at a conference nominated himself as a crusty feather pillow—his late-night calls sandblasted with jokes as jagged as the dried lava he smuggled out of Iceland in large black suitcases. Though she barely knew him, he surprised her by keeping track of her treatment schedule, inviting her round for watercress soup when she was in London, visiting her seaside town after her first chemo. Under chalk cliffs, she made tentative overtures, but he reacted like the small incurious horses in Hvolsvöllur, who hadn't even sniffed at the apples she'd offered under the pale midnight sun. Icelandic horses, the farmer chuckled the next day, didn't have a clue that apples were edible. As for the sculptor, she took him back to her flat to see her prize piece of Glit pottery, a heavy grey dish made of lava, scored with a rough topographical map of Iceland. She expected him to explore the lumps, peaks and crevices, but he held the bowl aloft and struck it with his thumbnail, making it ring. In his flat she fingered bells formed from extinguished volcanoes, silent instruments that spoke with tongues of dead fire. For months she feared dying, amputation, post-op agony—but then a mid-chemo MRI scan revealed her tumour had disappeared. He didn't believe in good news, and his caustic jokes intensified, but she laughed even when they chafed. Let him piss on her chips—she was getting better and her hair would grow back. *Do you want to watch the sunset over the river?* she asked. He stepped on to the jetty, donned a pair of black shades. She remembered the night they'd met—him drunk, pointing at the full moon, insisting everyone look at it. She still wasn't sure if the moon was a numinous eye, a cut apple, or a cloudy scar in the sky, and sometimes she wondered if people who loved Iceland were really in love with their own lonely pain.

After the Tumour Disappeared

i.m. Bart Moore-Gilbert

I was drifting down a side aisle in a church
as, one by one, members of the congregation rose
to intone a line each of a poem that impressed me
with its sonorous gravitas, though now I can't recall
a single word. In the dream I remembered
I'd been here before, with Bart, at this very service—
not his funeral, of course; an earlier ceremony,
together in the Lady Chapel, him in crumpled linens,
face lifted to the poem, me in chic red chemo cap
hissing to a woman, ". . . but *they* own all the halls."
I slipped into the pew behind us, quietly, unnoticed,
watched the friends we were embrace. Then
the congregation vanished. I walked on down the nave
as the church became a soaring sun-washed wall.

Homecoming

My Father's house holds many doors,
My Mother's garden knows no gate.

She plants her flowers in his floors,
Flings windows wide, calls . . . *not too late.*

I scale the crumbling midnight walls—
She warms the milk, he rolls the dates.

Night

O swollen black river
   crashing through earth
glistening sea-snake
   with iridescent scales
thrashing the borders
   of day's jurisdiction
carving dark channels
   into grey lunar
bedrock, your froth
   floods the banks
of reason and dream
   devours the ground
that was never solid
   beneath my cold feet
but though these months
   of steroidal insomnia
have not tamed you
   I've learned how to ride
your muscular currents
   float with the flotsam
you spew from your jaws—
   shadowy podcasts
forgotten sonatas
   breast-crawling elephants
dim islands of calm
   that carnival barker
with crepuscular stubble
   a tube of wasabi
tucked in his top hat
   to daub on my nipple
if we ever touch land

It Takes a Global Village

I cried bloody buckets,
you gave me flowers:
thirsty pink roses,
fierce gladioli,
blushing sweet Williams,
baby breath sprays—
I ran out of vases,
the flat looked like I'd died.
I picked myself up
from the petal-smeared floor,
and through swollen eyes
emailed you all,
asked for mangoes and comedies,
invites to meals
with anti-breast cancer menus,
massage gift certificates, patience
if you messaged and I didn't reply.
As I hovered in limbo,
scrubbing the kitchen
and vacuuming the ceiling,
first the postman knocked
with armfuls of cards,
lemongrass soap, poetry books;
then you, unannounced,
bearing frivolous novels
and philosophical questions,
colouring books
and rainbows of pens,
samphire and sea kale
foraged from Shoreham,
slender green wheatgrass
grown in your bathtub,
the comfort of apples
plucked from wild Sussex orchards
or nicked from a churchyard
just down the road.

As my torture grew closer,
you shopped, cooked and baked,
until my table was laden
with Moroccan lamb stew,
red pepper soups,
plantains and ginger,
kim chi, kombucha,
cranberry granola,
roast beef and chicken,
crispy Irish spuds,
Iranian salad with pomegranate seeds,
Mexican black bean burgers,
Caribbean comfort food—
red lentil dahl
and coconut spinach—
always a potful
with leftovers to freeze,
while under the table
you tucked boxes of beets
to chop for the juicer,
or serve with goat's cheese.
After each chemo, when
drugged to the gills,
achey and itchy,
metal-mouthed, watery-eyed,
I could just about drag
my skin-and-bone frame
from kettle to tap,
you opened your doors,
gave me languid stays
in eco-sanatoriums that would
turn Thomas Mann green:
book-lined spare rooms
lit by Bloomsbury lamps,
with views of the chimney pots
and your garden veg beds,

afternoons on sofas
cocooned in soft Persian throws,
festivals of comics and curry,
the Moomins and Pho;
and as my hair fell out
in erratic swathes,
you gave me Shea butter,
an African print headscarf
and wrapping tutorials.
When I got home
to my own cushions and quilts,
you zoomed down from London,
Oxford, Yorkshire and Lancs,
flew across the ocean
from Qualicum Beach,
brought fig-scented candles,
took me out for vegan lunch,
gave me Frankincense hand rubs,
drew pastel portraits
of my Buddhist-Alien head,
measured me up for a
Venus di Milo wax maquette,
left me tucked in
with *Wallace and Gromit*,
sipping Parisian tisanes.
How could I not rally,
know myself blessed?
When I blogged about my progress
your legions of comments,
smileys and hearts,
made me feel like the queen
of an ethereal realm.
Though just to make sure
I didn't forget
about the suffering of others,
you sent me *The Wire*,

and three famine novels
—Finnish history, Russian horror,
and South Korean noir—
while out there, the world,
not to be stumped,
chipped in with Brexit,
Aleppo and Trump . . .
For the days I managed
to stumble outside,
you gave me those massage vouchers;
a mini-trampoline
and four strong arms to assemble it;
a shoulder bag from Cape Town
that strangers admired;
you treated me to green juice
and gooey carrot cake;
took me on pilgrimages
to the stained glass of Rottingdean,
the clear glass of Berwick,
the sci-fi secrets of Midhurst,
a winter gathering of Muslims
beside Salisbury Cathedral;
together we walked
the gleaming white cliffs
that gave Albion its name.
As the days grew shorter
and the temperature plunged
you kept me warm
with a polka-dot scarf,
posh flannel pyjamas,
pink stripy socks,
and a Turkish tea towel
woven fine and large
as a shawl.
Though I didn't ask
you all for your prayers

you gave them too,
in churches and mosques,
pagan covens and camps,
you petitioned the Mystery
to please not take me back yet;
and in my faithless faith
in the journey we're on,
I thankfully received
meditation apps,
a mouse medicine totem
and a smoky quartz wand,
homeopathy pills
to counteract 'burning soles',
tree essence remedies
to help me prepare
for the operation to come,
a hypnotherapy CD
I played night after night,
its repeated insistence
on 'benefits and advantages'
blossoming beyond dreams
when those of you
not on my email list
gave me forgiveness
and apologies too.
All the while the flowers bloomed,
dazzling stargazers
that perfumed the room
with glamour and promise,
begonias and ivy
I planted out in fresh air.
As for the mangoes,
you cycled over in the cold
bearing two juicy sunsets,
whizzed them up in a sauce
with cumin and lime.

In return, at last,
I had a present for you—
miraculous news:
the chemo had worked.
I still had to have
six lymph nodes removed,
but my breast tissue
was lumpless—
the tumour was gone.
Now of course I thank
the doctors and drugs
for that vanishing act,
but in inching so close
to my own death,
I entered a truth
—ancient, electric—
that lit up a path
through a summer of despair,
a winter of fear:
the curing of cancer
may be a chemical boon,
but it was you, my family
of family and friends,
who gave me my life back,
gave me back to the world.

Post-op

for Marilyn Hacker

Outside, the clouds part
and a cold sun
silvers the sea. Inside,

as butterflies and swimming women
surrender the mantelpiece
to polar bear cubs and red berries,

I lie on the sofa reading the Qur'an,
a heart-shaped cushion
tucked under my arm.

Like caviar-hunters, the surgeons
have filleted my chest, scooped out
every last suspect cell;

their blue dye haloes my nipple—
for a year my breast will weep
lapis lazuli tears.

Online, a man
with eyes of dark fire
says he admires my courage.

I am not brave.
All I have done is submit
to the will of the seasons, embrace

an untranslatable change.

NOTES

'Two Emilys': The word totem is derived from the Algonquian (most likely Ojibwe) word odoodem [oˈtuːtɛm], meaning "his kinship group." Oolichan are candlefish and sta-bigs are gifts of preserved food wrapped in mats or storage baskets. Nuu-chah-nulth means 'to circle around'; spoken by the villagers of Yuquot to give directions to James Cook, the term is now used to refer to fifteen related First Peoples of the West Coast of Vancouver Island.

Emily Carr (1871–1945), iconic Canadian painter, is also the author of six memoirs detailing her friendships and relationship with the indigenous people of the Pacific Northwest, the first of which, *Klee Wyck*, won the 1941 Governor General's Award.

Emily Givner (1966–2004) was an accomplished writer and cellist. Her short story 'Canadian Mint', a winner in *The Toronto Star*'s summer fiction competition, appears in her posthumous collection *A Heart in Port* (Thistledown Press, 2007), which takes its title from a poem by Emily Dickinson.

'reQuesting': In 1995 an all-white jury returned a verdict of guilty of manslaughter in the case of the death of Pamela Jean George (age 28). According to Blaine Favel, the then Chief of the Federation of Saskatchewan Indian Nations, the verdict was "one of the most unjust in Saskatchewan judicial history".

Beverley Jacobs of the Mohawk Nation, in her then role as President of the Native Women's Association of Canada, spoke in parliament with other Aboriginal leaders to respond to Canada's 2008 National Apology to Inuit, First Nations and Metis people of Canada. The full Apology and Response can be viewed at: http://www.cpac.ca/en/programs/cpac-special/episodes/14636034.

'Tekahionwake': Kanien'kehá:ka (Mohawk) is an Iroquoian language of the Northeast Woodlands. It is the healthiest of the Six Nations languages of Ontario, with about three thousand fluent speakers, half in Canada and half in New York state.

Tekahionwake ('double wampum') was the Mohawk name of poet, writer and performer E. Pauline Johnson (1862–1913), daughter of Onwanonsyshon, Head Chief of the Six Nations, and Emily S. Howells, a British-born relative of the American novelist W.D. Howells. Although Tekahionwake was written out of Canadian literary history, the recent publication of two biographies and the production of the opera *Pauline* (2014), with a libretto by Margaret Atwood, have reignited interest in her life and work.

'True Patriot Love': *Tales from the Smokehouse* (McClelland and Stewart, 1999) is a collection of erotic First Nations stories, collected by Herbert Schwarz and illustrated by Daphne Odjig (1919–2016), an eminent Canadian First Nations artist of Odawa-Potawatomi-English heritage. Joyce Weiland (1930–1998) was a Canadian mixed media artist and experimental filmaker of British heritage.

The saskatoon berry derives its name from an anglicization of the Cree language word misâskwatômina (mis-sack-qua-too-mina), which means "the fruit of the tree of many branches". The word is also the source of the city name Saskatoon, which is located on the banks of the South Saskatchewan River, an anglicization of Kisiskatchewani Sipi, meaning 'swiftly flowing river'.

'Eva Gore-Booth and Con Markievicz Gently Chide an Old Friend': The Gore-Booth sisters, Eva and Constance, were childhood friends of W.B. Yeats, who famously mourned their transformation into political activists. Constance, who married a Polish count, took part in the Easter Rising and was only spared execution due to her gender. Eva moved to England where she wrote poetry, defended the rights of itinerant female labourers, and became a quiet icon of the Irish LGBT community.

'Ahed': In December 2017, following a protest during which her cousin was shot in the head by a rubber bullet and severely wounded, Ahed Tamimi, a 16-year-old Palestinian activist from the Occupied West Bank, was arrested for slapping a soldier. Sentenced to eight months in jail, she was released in July 2018.

'An Aisling': The aisling (ASH-ling) is a genre of Irish poetry, a 'vision poem' in which Ireland appears to the poet in the form of a woman. Florence Crawford (1931-2011), a resident of West Belfast, was a shop worker, avid reader and single mother to Mairtín Crawford (1967–2004), one of the most significant Northern Irish literary figures of his generation. A poet, journalist, editor and live literature organiser, Mairtín is remembered in the Belfast Book Festival's annual Mairtín Crawford Award for Poetry and for Short Story.

'Indelible': On June 1, 2018, Razan al-Najjar, a 21-year-old volunteer paramedic, was killed by an Israeli sniper while tending to the wounded at a demonstration on the eastern border of Gaza. She was the 119th Palestinian to be killed during the Great March of Return, a series of weekly protests which calls for Israel to lift its eleven-year siege on Gaza and allow Palestinian refugees to return to their villages and towns. Over 10,000 Palestinians have been injured during the March of Return, and the death toll has, at time of writing (November 2018), risen to over 150. During this period Israeli media reported that one Israeli soldier was moderately injured due to shrapnel from a grenade thrown by a Palestinian from inside Gaza and, outside of the context of the protests, one Israeli soldier was killed by Palestinian sniper fire near the fence that separates Gaza and Israel.

'Shaking the Bottle': On September 22, 2004, Zainab Abu Salem, an 18-year-old children's television presenter from the Askar refugee camp near Nablus in the West Bank, detonated a suicide bomb in Jerusalem, an action praised in Al-fatah, a Hamas children's newspaper. Directly after the bombing, the Israeli Defence Force bulldozed Abu Salem's family home.

'The Purse': In October 2015, Dareen Tatour, a 33-year-old Palestinian poet and photographer from Reineh in the Galilee, was arrested over social media posts and a poem, 'Resist, My People, Resist Them'. During her trial, which took nearly three years, Tatour was held under house arrest or in prison. In the summer of 2018 she was convicted of incitement and sentenced to five months in jail. Released in October 2018, she is currently working on poems written in prison, and on collaborations with musicians and theatre artists including the Israeli playwright Einat Weizman.

'Adamantine': The story of Elisabeth Fritzl, an Austrian woman held captive by her father in the cellar of the family home for 24 years, has been extensively covered in the world media. An account of Adelheid Kastner's psychiatric report on Josef Fritzl is available at: https://www.the guardian.com/world/2009/mar/19/fritzl-psychiatrist-verdict.

'Don't Count Your Lumpectomies': Eva Saulitis (1964–2016) was a highly regarded poet, essayist, and marine biologist. Her posthumous collection of essays, *Becoming Earth* (Boreal Books, 2016), explores the profound relationship between cancer and the natural world.

While this transatlantic collection was typeset in California and contains poems set in Canada, British spelling and punctuation conventions are used throughout to reflect the author's current domicile.

BIOGRAPHICAL NOTE

Naomi Foyle is a British-Canadian poet, essayist, verse dramatist and novelist. Her poetry has appeared in journals and anthologies including *Poetry Review*, the *London Magazine*, *Poetry Ireland Review*, and *The Poetry of Sex* (Viking/Penguin). Her debut collection, *The Night Pavilion*, an Autumn 2008 Poetry Book Society Recommendation, was followed by *The World Cup* and five science fiction novels. Also the editor of *A Blade of Grass: New Palestinian Poetry*, Naomi Foyle lives in Brighton, UK, and lectures at the University of Chichester. Among her many accolades, she was awarded the 2014 Hryhorii Skovoroda Prize for her poetry and essays about Ukraine.